Irish Independent

QUIZ BOOK

GW00371955

Irish Independent

QUIZ BOOK

CATHERINE TROY

Gill & Macmillan

Gill & Macmillan Ltd
Hume Avenue, Park West, Dublin 12
with associated companies throughout the world
www.gillmacmillan.ie
© Catherine Troy 2006
ISBN-13: 978 07171 3811 1
ISBN-10: 0 7171 3811 9
Print origination by TypeIT, Dublin
Printed by Nørhaven Paperback A/S, Denmark

This book is typeset in 10pt Palatino on 12pt.

The paper used in this book comes from the wood pulp
of managed forests. For every tree felled, at least one
tree is planted, thereby renewing natural resources.

A CIP catalogue record for this book is available from
the British Library.

1 3 5 4 2

Contents

Questions

Question Time 1

1. How many chambers are in the human heart?

2. Name the six counties of Northern Ireland.

3. What is the highest rank in the Irish army?

4. What sort of guitar did Jimi Hendrix play?

5. Where did Jesus turn water into wine at a marriage?

Question Time 2

1. What was the month and year of the assassination of President John F. Kennedy?

2. Which sheikdom is controlled by the horse-racing Maktoum family?

3. Who is the most widely syndicated cartoonist in history?

4. Desdemona was a character in which of Shakespeare's plays?

5. What are the three primary colours?

Answers on page 93

Question Time 3

1. Which four Irishmen were awarded Nobel Prizes for literature between 1923 and 1995?

2. What are the Northern Lights also known as?

3. Who were the two founders of Microsoft?

4. On which part of the body would you have a tracheotomy?

5. What colour are pistachio nuts?

Question Time 4

1. How many teeth does an adult human have?

2. Which country has on record the highest per capita consumption of alcohol?

3. Who produced the film *Gone with the Wind*?

4. What is the fastest class of sail boat?

5. Which golfer has won the most Majors?

Answers on page 93

Question Time 5

1. What American town is the home of Coca-Cola?

2. What is the name of the boy who befriended E.T. in *E.T, the Extra-Terrestrial*?

3. Who led the first Labour government in Britain?

4. Which plant is associated with St Patrick's Day?

5. What was Pope John Paul II's original name?

Question Time 6

1. Who were the two military leaders of the Easter Rising?

2. Who wrote the *Foundation* trilogy of sci-fi novels?

3. In which continent would you find the Apennines?

4. Who wrote the poem *The Lady of the Lake?*

5. What does a taxidermist do?

Answers on page 94

Question Time 7

1. If an egg floats on water, is it fresh or stale?

2. What are the four most commonly spoken languages of the world?

3. On the Mohs scale, what is the hardest mineral?

4. What was Britain's first winning entry in the Eurovision Song Contest?

5. Who discovered the nucleus of the atom?

Question Time 8

1. What is the world's most sparsely populated country?

2. Which world famous novel records a day in the life of an advertising salesman on 16 June 1904?

3. In which year did Elvis Presley die?

4. Who was the first man to reach the North Pole?

5. What kind of fruit are Green Williams?

Answers on page 94

Question Time 9

1. Name the two tramps in Beckett's play *Waiting for Godot*.

2. Which country won the first World Cup in soccer?

3. In which country would you find the Atlas Mountains?

4. Where was Lyndon B. Johnson sworn in as US President?

5. Who was Pope for just 33 days?

Question Time 10

1. What is the first commandment?

2. Prior to its break-up, what was the world's largest country?

3. What tunnel did the French and Italian complete in 1962?

4. Who wrote 'Ode to the West Wind'?

5. What is the capital of Australia?

Answers on page 95

Question Time 11

1. What was the subject of Charles Darwin's famous theory?

2. Which is the second planet from the sun?

3. Who in 1837 invented the steel plough?

4. Which race has a distance of 26 miles and 385 yards?

5. What is tofu made from?

Question Time 12

1. What fruit can be classed as beef, cherry or plum?

2. Where might you find a finial, a chevet and a slype?

3. Who wrote *The Female Eunuch*?

4. Which country was the first to grant women the vote?

5. How many of his wives did Henry VIII divorce?

Answers on page 95

Question Time 13

1. According to the Bible, who shall inherit the earth?

2. Which plant is the national emblem of Wales?

3. In which Irish city would you find the Spanish Arch?

4. Which enemy of Batman usually carries an umbrella?

5. Which Washington edifice has 898 steps?

Question Time 14

1. A nuncio represents which state?

2. Which Dire Straits album became the first million-selling CD?

3. Which novel by Jane Austen was originally called *First Impressions*?

4. Which Middle Ages heroine was born at Domrémy, France?

5. Which state did the Americans buy from the Russians?

Answers on page 96

Question Time 15

1. On what day of the year particularly do you eat pancakes?

2. In which county is the Giant's Causeway?

3. Where is the Empire State building?

4. What is the largest species of shark?

5. What name is given to a population count?

Question Time 16

1. What star sign was Jesus Christ?

2. Which three US states start with the letter O?

3. How many planets are in the solar system?

4. Au is the scientific symbol of which element?

5. Which composer had the middle name Amadeus?

Question Time 17

1. The mistral winds blow from which mountains?

2. Mohair is the fleece of what animal?

3. Which chemical formula is represented by CO?

4. Members of which religious group consume 'Kosher' food?

5. Which Scottish hero travelled under the name of Betty Burke?

Question Time 18

1. What is the largest stringed instrument?

2. Which sport uses granites?

3. How many Ice Ages were there in the Pliocene era?

4. What animal is reputed to be the longest domesticated?

5. Which country includes William Tell among its national heroes?

Answers on page 97

Question Time 19

1. In what year was Ireland declared a republic?

2. In which country is Darjeeling tea grown?

3. What type of animal is an ortolan?

4. How many days are there in Lent?

5. Which is the largest of the four provinces of Ireland?

Question Time 20

1. How much does a litre of water weigh?

2. With which religion are the Jesuits associated?

3. In which sport is a long-horse used?

4. Which British biologist founded and named the science of genetics?

5. Give or take 500 million years, how old is the earth?

Answers on page 97

Question Time 21

1. Who invented the mercury thermometer?

2. What did Karl Benz name after his daughter?

3. With which Irish town do you associate John B. Keane?

4. What is the collective term for a group of leopards?

5. Name the six counties of Munster.

Question Time 22

1. What major world event lasted from 1939 to 1945?

2. What did Charles Lindbergh call his Atlantic-crossing plane?

3. Fair Isle is off the coast of where?

4. Who discovered penicillin?

5. In a Punch and Judy show, what sort of animal is Toby?

Answers on page 98

Question Time 23

1. Name Horatio Nelson's last battle.

2. Which jockey rode Nijinsky to win the Derby in 1970?

3. In which county are the Cliffs of Moher?

4. Who had a hit with the album *Graceland*?

5. Which is bigger: a rabbit or a hare?

Question Time 24

1. Which beautiful blonde starred in *The Seven Year Itch*?

2. Does cheesecake contain cheese?

3. Red Rum set a record time for winning the Grand National. Was it seven, eight or nine minutes?

4. What is the value of Roman numeral XV?

5. What is a one thousand millionth of a second called?

Answers on page 98

Question Time 25

1. 1,000 Guineas, 2,000 Guineas, The Oaks, St Leger. Name the missing classic horse race.

2. Where is the Sea of Tranquillity?

3. Who was reputed to be the fastest mouse in all of Mexico?

4. Which day of the week is named after a Roman god?

5. Who played Basil Fawlty in *Fawlty Towers*?

Question Time 26

1. What flower is nicknamed goldilocks?

2. Name the three stands in Croke Park before it was re-developed.

3. Name the South American driver who won the most motor-racing world championships.

4. In which direction do the trade winds blow?

5. What is the chemical name for vinegar?

Answers on page 99

Question Time 27

1. When was the Berlin Wall built?

2. Which bird's name means two under par in golf?

3. Which famous dance hall was opened in Paris in 1900?

4. Where was the Minoan civilisation?

5. Who was the first president of Ireland?

Question Time 28

1. Name the two kings at the Battle of the Boyne.

2. How many animals are there in the Chinese calendar?

3. What nationality is the operatic tenor Placido Domingo?

4. Who first reached the South Pole?

5. Who wrote *Little Women*?

Answers on page 99

Question Time 29

1. In which town in Ireland did Cromwell's first massacre take place?

2. Who was the first British Labour prime minister with an overall majority?

3. Which capital city stands on the Manzanares river?

4. Who wrote *A Day in the Life of Ivan Denisovich*?

5. What type of creature is a nutcracker?

Question Time 30

1. *The Two Towers* is the second book in which trilogy?

2. Which river flows into the sea at New York City?

3. Who is sometimes known as the godfather of soul?

4. Females have two X chromosomes: true or false?

5. Who was responsible for the reform of the Carmelite order, and died in 1582?

Answers on page 100

Question Time 31

1. What is the capital of Canada?

2. Orange pekoe is a variety of what?

3. Which US city stands on the Potomac river?

4. Who composed the *Moonlight Sonata?*

5. To which animal family do martens belong?

Question Time 32

1. Waitangi Day is a national holiday in which country?

2. What racecourse is home to the Kentucky Derby?

3. What is the smallest interval on a piano called?

4. Who is the patron saint of Spain, a virgin martyr whose emblem is a lamb?

5. When was the Berlin Wall pulled down?

Answers on page 100

Question Time 33

1. In which hemisphere would you find the Aurora Australia: northern or southern?

2. What is the home of a hare called?

3. The Opium Wars in the Far East were mainly between which two countries?

4. Who was the Merchant of Venice in Shakespeare's play?

5. What is the state capital of Hawaii?

Question Time 34

1. Whom did Jimmy Carter succeed as president of the USA?

2. What major race is run at Longchamp?

3. What kind of creature is a flying fox?

4. Who gave Victoria Falls its name?

5. On what date is St Swithin's Day?

Answers on page 101

Question Time 35

1. Who was the youngest ever US president?

2. What is the boundary of a circle called?

3. Which country declared war on Britain on 18 June 1812?

4. Who was the Moor of Venice in Shakespeare's play?

5. What is the state capital of California?

Question Time 36

1. Whom did Margaret Thatcher succeed as prime minister?

2. Who wrote the celebrated book *Diana, Her True Story*?

3. What is the gambling slang for £500 or $500?

4. What is the largest country in Africa?

5. In what month does the Chelsea Flower Show normally take place?

Answers on page 101

Question Time 37

1. Which name, from an Italian city, is also a name of a two/three flavoured ice cream?

2. Which Greek philosopher was taught by Socrates and in turn taught Aristotle?

3. Name the divisions of the legal year known as sittings.

4. A mercer would have traded in what type of goods?

5. *The Scream* is a famous work by which artist?

Question Time 38

1. In the Bible, how many days was Jesus in the tomb?

2. What is a mendicant?

3. What name was given to Cromwell's cavalry troopers in the English Civil War?

4. What do onomasticians study?

5. What is the oldest known alcoholic drink, made from honey?

Answers on page 102

Question Time 39

1. Where in Ireland are the Curragh and the Bog of Allen?

2. What was the innovative feature of the Rolex 'Oyster' watch?

3. What are the Yeomen of the Tower of London called?

4. What ingredient forms the topping on crème brûlée?

5. What is monotheism?

Question Time 40

1. What is the British election system called?

2. What is the name of the ghost ship that reputedly haunts the Cape of Good Hope?

3 Which is the first of the *Canterbury Tales*?

4. From which plant is the heart-drug digitalis obtained?

5. In which county is Stansted airport?

Answers on page 102

Question Time 41

1. From which cereal does sweetcorn come?

2. How tall, to the nearest inch, is an Oscar statuette?

3. Rembrandt painted *The Laughing Cavalier*: true or false?

4. Niagara Falls is between which two Great Lakes?

5. How many lines in a sonnet?

Question Time 42

1. Which is the world's largest gulf?

2. In the nursery rhyme, what was the only tune that Tom, the piper's son, could play?

3. Which railway station in the UK has a fictional bear named after it?

4. Which city used to be called New Amsterdam?

5. To which parts of the human body does the word volar relate?

Answers on page 103

Question Time 43

1. What is the name commonly given to the northern parts of Scandinavia and the Kola Peninsula in Russia, traditionally inhabited by the Sami people?

2. In the nursery rhyme 'Pease Porridge Hot', how old was the porridge?

3. Which Christine nearly brought down the British government in the Profumo scandal in 1963?

4. In music, the viola is the alto member of which family of instruments?

5. What is the hardest substance in the human body?

Question Time 44

1. Which South American country is named after the line of latitude that runs through it?

2. What are Kerrs Pinks and Maris Pipers?

3. John Galliano is famous as what?

4. Chuck Yeager was the first pilot to break what?

5. How long is a tennis court from baseline to baseline?

Answers on page 103

Question Time 45

1. Which South American country took its name from the Latin for 'silvery'?

2. What was the first name of the British explorer Captain Cook?

3. What type of food is Edam?

4. From which poem are these lines, 'Laugh, and the world laughs with you; weep, and you weep alone'?

5. How high is the net on a tennis court, at the centre?

Question Time 46

1. All horses have the same official birthday: true or false?

2. What is a violinist's bow string made of?

3. What river does the Hoover Dam stand on?

4. What is removal of tissue from a living body for diagnostic purposes called?

5. How is 2,000 written in Roman numerals?

Answers on page 104

Question Time 47

1. What is the correct title of the daughter of an earl, marquis or duke?

2. In which country are the ruins of Troy?

3. From what city does the Mariinsky (formerly Kirov) Ballet come?

4. What are the highest odds paid by a casino in a roulette frame?

5. What is the most sacred river in India?

Question Time 48

1. Brisbane is the capital of which Australian state?

2. How many ventricles are there in the human heart?

3. To which country does the island of Crete belong?

4. Who founded what is now the Royal Ballet?

5. What is the highest score possible from a single stroke at billiards?

Answers on page 104

Question Time 49

1. Amnesia is a medical term for loss of what?

2. In which field of the arts did Jacob Epstein achieve fame?

3. Who directed the film *Apocalypse Now*?

4. Which war did the Potsdam Conference follow?

5. Which mythical figure was chained to a mountain where an eagle tore at his liver every day?

Question Time 50

1. A haemogram is a medical test of what?

2. Which is the world's largest navigable lake?

3. In which country was the Boxer Rebellion?

4. Who is the subject of Irving Stone's *Lust for Life*?

5. What caused over 20 million deaths worldwide in the years 1918 and 1919?

Answers on page 105

Question Time 51

1. Which English king was beheaded in 1649?

2. In which sport are there positions called 'props' and 'locks'?

3. Name the novelist who wrote *Amongst Women*.

4. The pulmonary artery connects which organ to the heart?

5. What is the longest river in Italy?

Question Time 52

1. From which Apollo mission was Neil Armstrong when he walked on the moon in 1969?

2. In history, which Russian leader's name means 'man of steel'?

3. What is Eva Herzigova famous for modelling?

4. The holiday resort of Sliema is on which Mediterranean island?

5. Which Irish band had a world hit with the song 'Fire'?

Answers on page 105

Question Time 53

1. Which adult male singing voice is lower than a tenor but higher than a bass?

2. York, white and red are types of what vegetable?

3. What was the name of Shakespeare's only son?

4. The Faroe Islands belong to which Scandinavian country?

5. What is the capital of the US state of Indiana?

Question Time 54

1. Which twentieth-century Anglo-American poet wrote about 'Rannoch, by Glencoe'?

2. In which county are Ballymena and Ballymoney?

3. What is the title of Oscar Wilde's only novel?

4. Who played the male lead in *Mary Poppins*?

5. What nationality was the boxer Rocky Marciano?

Answers on page 106

Question Time 55

1. Does a stalagmite grow up or down?

2. What is the name of the principal performer of *Riverdance* and *Lord of the Dance*?

3. Who wrote *A Farewell to Arms*?

4. Where is the San Andreas Fault?

5. A candela is a unit which measures the intensity of what?

Question Time 56

1. What is the smallest state in the world?

2. What is the capital of Sierra Leone?

3. What kind of plane was a Lancaster?

4. Which famous Irishman was killed at the Battle of Landen in 1693?

5. Mount Everest is in which mountain range?

Answers on page 106

Question Time 57

1. Who wrote the *Mallen* trilogy of novels?

2. In what city was the Irish Unionist Edward Carson born?

3. Who wrote the story of *The Ugly Duckling*?

4. Gnocchi is a food from Italy. What is it?

5. Geronimo was a chief of which Native American tribe?

Question Time 58

1. Which insect group includes soldiers, robbers and slaves?

2. What is the capital of Jamaica?

3. Which country developed Mirage warplanes?

4. From George Washington to George W. Bush, and including both, how many US presidents have there been?

5. In which comic is Desperate Dan?

Answers on page 107

Question Time 59

1. In the Bible, which book follows the four gospels?

2. In music, how many notes has a scale?

3. In which year did the Easter Rising take place?

4. Scotch and wych are two species of which tree?

5. Who invented television?

Question Time 60

1. How many parts of alloy has 18-carat gold?

2. On a three-masted vessel, what is the mizzen mast?

3. Name Adam and Eve's three sons.

4. How many colours are there in a rainbow?

5. In which country is Lusaka?

Answers on page 107

Question Time 61

1. What trophy is awarded to the All-Ireland Senior Football champions?

2. What is the name of that part of the small intestine leading from the stomach?

3. In sailing, how many masts has a yacht?

4. Setanta was the boyhood name of what legendary hero?

5. Badwater is the western hemisphere's lowest point. Where is it?

Question Time 62

1. How many letters are in the alphabet?

2. Who wrote the novel *Captain Corelli's Mandolin*?

3. In which county is Whiddy Island?

4. What is the official title of the United States foreign minister?

5. In which year did George V become King of England?

Answers on page 108

Question Time 63

1. What is the capital of Latvia?

2. What is a Suffolk Punch?

3. How many volleyball players are there on each team?

4. Who directed the film *Excalibur*?

5. On which side of the road do cars drive in Japan?

Question Time 64

1. In which Jane Austen novel would you find the Dashwood sisters?

2. How many countries originally joined the European Monetary Union?

3. In US currency, how many cents are there in a nickel?

4. Where would you hear Gregorian chant?

5. In Northern Ireland, what do the initials UDR stand for?

Answers on page 108

Question Time 65

1. How many psalms are in the Book of Psalms?

2. What does a lexicographer make?

3. What pain-killer is derived from the bark of a willow tree?

4. Who won the men's singles at Wimbledon in 1993, 1994 and 1998?

5. How do frogs breathe under water?

Question Time 66

1. Which queen's divorce features in Shakespeare's *Henry VIII*?

2. Name the eye disease which clouds the lens.

3. What Hindi word means both curtain and seclusion of women?

4. Who wrote *A Tale of a Tub* in 1704?

5. What is the only internal human organ that can reproduce itself?

Answers on page 109

Question Time 67

1. In *Hamlet*, whose grave was being dug when Yorrick's skull was unearthed?

2. Where is the jugular vein?

3. What is the Islamic word for holy war?

4. Who wrote *Rich Man, Poor Man*?

5. Who in 1985 became the youngest world chess champion ever?

Question Time 68

1. What is baccarat?

2. What does a haematologist study?

3. What do you need to sup with the devil?

4. What sort of music did Ira D. Sankey compose?

5. Who was head of the German SS?

Answers on page 109

Question Time 69

1. By what name is scorpion grass better known?

2. Where would you find the Dewey decimal system in use?

3. In the Bible, who wrote the Epistles?

4. Where is the *Midland Tribune* published?

5. What is the name of the children's construction kits which consist of metal strips, screws, nuts and bolts, etc?

Question Time 70

1. What is a ducat?

2. Who wrote, 'When a man is tired of London, he is tired of life, for there is in London all life can afford'?

3. Which number in bingo is called half a crown?

4. What shipping forecast area lies between Faeroes and Viking?

5. Who opened the first British birth control clinic?

Answers on page 110

Question Time 71

1. What flower has the same name as a reddish orange mineral sometimes used as a gem?

2. Where would you find the Pleiades and what are they?

3. Which literary person in his will left his wife his furniture and his second-best bed?

4. Where is the *Kilkenny People* published?

5. The town of Ghent is in which country?

Question Time 72

1. Which singer was watching the detectives?

2. George Orwell developed what thought process in his novel *1984*?

3. How many pieces does each side have in draughts?

4. Which Irish ghost is said to wail outside houses where death is imminent?

5. Where in London would you see the White Tower?

Answers on page 110

Question Time 73

1. What is the voting age in Ireland?

2. What is the historical name for a woman's long, double-breasted outer garment, with skirts often cut away in front?

3. Who would use an étrier or a chockstone?

4. What is the name of the French national anthem?

5. What is the title of the highest ranking British judge in the Court of Appeal?

Question Time 74

1. In which year did James Dean die?

2. Name the loose over-garment prescribed by law, worn by Jews in the Middle Ages.

3. In which sporting event do the winners move *backwards*?

4. What is the value of Roman numeral MCMLXXXIV?

5. How should the Bishop of London be formally addressed?

Answers on page 111

Question Time 75

1. Which river flows through Lisbon?

2. What does GDP stand for?

3. Which ball game is peculiar to Eton College?

4. From which area of Spain was Don Quixote?

5. What is Canada's official emblem?

Question Time 76

1. Moscow stands on which river?

2. What nationality was Marie Curie?

3. What does a gamophobe fear?

4. Who wrote the novel *Tom Jones*?

5. What is the green-eyed monster?

Answers on page 111

Question Time 77

1. In the Old Testament, what book comes between Genesis and Leviticus?

2. What is the capital of New York state?

3. Who phoned Neil Armstrong on his first walk on the moon?

4. In the comic, where did Desperate Dan live?

5. Where is the Bay of Plenty?

Question Time 78

1. What name is given to the study of the properties and distribution of water?

2. Where is your epiglottis?

3. Which British reformer was known as the Great Commoner?

4. Name the largest of the Greek islands.

5. Of which novel is Fanny Price the heroine?

Answers on page 112

Question Time 79

1. What name is given to the art of working metals?

2. Name the oldest city in Germany, on the banks of the Rhine.

3. Who created Frankenstein?

4. Which racing circuit has a bend called Paddock?

5. Name Switzerland's largest city.

Question Time 80

1. Name the fifth book of the Old Testament.

2. Who followed Nelson Mandela as president of South Africa?

3. Spider, hermit and masked are all what?

4. What piece of jewellery is a half hunter?

5. What is a double bogey in golf?

Answers on page 112

Question Time 81

1. What is the only miracle mentioned in all four gospels?

2. What is the unit of currency in Norway?

3. What kind of creature is a copperhead?

4. Where are the Scottish Highland Games held?

5. What type of animal is a Wessex Saddleback?

Question Time 82

1. How many years is a coral anniversary?

2. Which literary character's favourite expression was 'Off with his head'?

3. Who wrote the British national anthem, 'God save the King'?

4. What was the Christian name of Hardy of Laurel and Hardy fame?

5. Proverbially, when is the darkest hour?

Answers on page 113

Question Time 83

1. What is celebrated on 7 January in the Russian Orthodox Church?

2. Which Thomas Hardy novel ends, 'As soon as they had strength they arose, joined hands again and went on'?

3. 'Strike up the band' was written by which American composer and pianist and his brother?

4. What was Stan Laurel's surname at birth?

5. Which British prime minister started his political career in 1900 as the successful Tory MP for Oldham?

Question Time 84

1. Which Shakespeare play begins, 'When shall we three meet again'?

2. What does the shoat grow up to become?

3. What did Kirkpatrick MacMillan invent in 1839?

4. What is the monetary unit of Singapore?

5. What kind of creature is a barbastelle?

Answers on page 113

Question Time 85

1. Which Shakespeare play begins, 'If music be the food of love'?

2. What is a female donkey called?

3. Who invented the hot-air balloon?

4. What is the monetary unit of Tunisia?

5. What is a pochard?

Question Time 86

1. 'Lily the Pink' was a hit for which trio?

2. Who won four gold medals in the 1936 Berlin Olympics?

3. According to the Bible, who was the father of the Jews?

4. Who followed Lyndon B. Johnson as President of the United States?

5. What battle was fought near Brussels on 18 June 1815?

Answers on page 114

Question Time 87

1. Napoleon was banished to which island?

2. What type of food is Rocquefort?

3. Which part of the body would suffer from trichosis?

4. Which explorer discovered Newfoundland in 1497?

5. What is sodium hydroxide commonly known as?

Question Time 88

1. Which book is the number one bestseller in the world?

2. Of which country was Juan Peron president?

3. What sort of garment is a Sloppy Joe?

4. Who was credited with the quotation, 'I never hated a man enough to give him his diamonds back'?

5. Who was Walt Whitman?

Answers on page 114

Question Time 89

1. Which part of the body is affected by Crohn's disease?

2. For which delicacy is Clarinbridge, Co. Galway famous?

3. Which football team is nicknamed the Hatters?

4. The Gutenberg Bible was printed in which German city?

5. What is hydrated magnesium sulphate commonly known as?

Question Time 90

1. Name the author of *War and Remembrance*.

2. What is the date of Scotland's national day?

3. In which novel does the ship *Pequod* appear?

4. What was Thomas Crapper's claim to fame?

5. What in chess was Deep Blue?

Answers on page 115

Question Time 91

1. Which Australian city was named after the father of the theory of evolution?

2. Who murdered Lord Louis Mountbatten in Sligo?

3. Who wrote the opera *Tosca*?

4. Who founded the Habitat design empire?

5. What is a young kangaroo called?

Question Time 92

1. Who, when asked what his golf handicap was, replied, 'I'm a one-eyed Jewish negro'?

2. Who was the first Roman Catholic president of the United States?

3. What kind of animal was Pinocchio's pet, Figaro?

4. Who wrote the ballet *The Nutcracker*?

5. Manque and Passe are terms in what gambling game?

Question Time 93

1. Name the Irish architect who designed the Custom House.

2. How many strings has a cello?

3. What is the capital of Chile?

4. The fox-hunting season covers which months?

5. What is studied by a heliologist?

Question Time 94

1. Who sang the number one hit 'Silver Lady'?

2. What is the disc or halo around the sun called?

3. What is known as the Queen amongst cocktail drinks?

4. Which British driver won the 1962 Grand Prix world championship in a BRM?

5. Which venomous serpent is also known as the pit viper?

Answers on page 116

Question Time 95

1. Name the author of *The Thorn Birds*.

2. What colour was the racehorse Arkle?

3. Which Shakespeare play had the alternative title *What You Will*?

4. Under which tree is the Buddha supposed to have sat when he attained enlightenment?

5. What is another name for a natatorium?

Question Time 96

1. What was David Livingstone's calling when he began his travels in Africa?

2. Which popular British romantic film featured the number one hit 'Love is all around'?

3. What government figure would you contact if you had problems with officialdom?

4. Who beat Red Rum in his final attempt at three in a row in the Grand National?

5. From which Italian city did FIAT originate?

Answers on page 116

Question Time 97

1. Which famous American comedian quipped, 'President Johnson says a war isn't really a war without my jokes'?

2. After which American president is the capital of Liberia named?

3. Which country lies between Algeria and Libya?

4. Which liner was the last holder of the Atlantic Blue Riband?

5. With how many backgammon pieces does each player start the game?

Question Time 98

1. Which is the only bird in the Chinese calendar?

2. Who played the title role in *Forrest Gump*?

3. In which American state is Fort Knox?

4. Who wrote the poem 'The Rolling English Road'?

5. Who described religion as 'the opium of the people'?

Answers on page 117

Question Time 99

1. Who was the mother of John the Baptist?

2. What is the capital of Vietnam?

3. In 1978, the Archbishop of Cracow succeeded to what office?

4. What is a bridewell?

5. Which bird lays the largest eggs in proportion to its size?

Question Time 100

1. After whom was the soccer World Cup trophy named?

2. Which European city is known as The Bride of the Sea?

3. In sport, which game has the largest playing pitch?

4. What would an Australian call strides?

5. Who wrote *Death in Venice*?

Answers on page 117

Question Time 101

1. Which was the only full-scale naval battle of World War One?

2. Who played the title role in the film *The Elephant Man*?

3. Which nationality was El Cid?

4. Which English cathedral has the oldest surviving working clock in the world?

5. Where are the Maldive Islands?

Question Time 102

1. Who was the emperor of China when Marco Polo visited his court?

2. To whom was Natalie Wood married when she died?

3. Who, with his twin Remus, was suckled by a wolf?

4. What is the study of fossils called?

5. To which family of birds does the robin belong?

Answers on page 118

Question Time 103

1. What were the adventurers Baffin, Frobisher and Franklin all searching for?

2. Rococo and baroque are styles of what?

3. Which day of the week is named after the Norse goddess of love?

4. What branch of science is called after the Greek for house?

5. Which international border is crossed most frequently?

Question Time 104

1. Who sang 'When will I see you again?'

2. Which planet is farthest from the sun?

3. Name the blind Benedictine monk who invented the first true sparkling champagne.

4. Which world champion racing driver was born in Milton, Dunbartonshire?

5. Which animal is considered to be the tallest?

Answers on page 118

Question Time 105

1. Who was King Lear's loyal daughter?

2. What is a dipsomaniac?

3. Where is the headquarters of the World Health Organisation?

4. In America, what is a cayuse?

5. What did Doctor Bobs and Bill W found in June 1935?

Question Time 106

1. Which poet popularised the limerick?

2. What term applies to space devoid of matter?

3. What is the name of the pre-match war dance performed by the New Zealand rugby team?

4. Which Asian country has the other name of Bharat?

5. What has to be produced in a writ of Habeas Corpus?

Answers on page 119

Question Time 107

1. Who is the mother of actresses Natasha and Joely Richardson?

2. Which countries are connected by the Brenner Pass?

3. Rioja wines are produced in which country?

4. What was Dirty Harry's surname in the series of films starring Clint Eastwood?

5. Which queen married William of Orange?

Question Time 108

1. What was the nationality of the astronomer Copernicus?

2. How many even numbers above zero are there on a roulette wheel?

3. Who wrote *20,000 Leagues under the Sea*?

4. Who directed the classic 1941 version of the film *The Maltese Falcon*?

5. What name is given to a wine bottle eight to twelve times its ordinary size?

Answers on page 119

Question Time 109

1. What kind of animal is a margay?

2. Which sea is connected to the Baltic Sea by the Kiel Canal?

3. Who painted *The Light of the World*?

4. Where is home to Noddy?

5. What is the capital of Trinidad?

Question Time 110

1. What would happen if you took an emetic medicine?

2. Name the three South American countries on the Equator.

3. Name the five Marx Brothers.

4. Which puppet series sprang out of *Sesame Street*?

5. Which king married Mary of Teck (Queen Mary)?

Answers on page 120

Question Time 111

1. Which day follows Shrove Tuesday?

2. What number is directly opposite nineteen on a dart board?

3. Who are thespians?

4. Name the Polish film director with a taste for the macabre as in *Rosemary's Baby*.

5. What is made only from pinot, meunier and chardonnay grapes?

Question Time 112

1. What is the most poisonous fish in the world?

2. Anne Hathaway was married to which famous writer?

3. Bayern is the German name for which region of Germany?

4. Where is home to the Flintstones?

5. What do the stripes on an American flag represent?

Answers on page 120

Question Time 113

1. What is also known as Hansen's disease?

2. In which country is Valparaiso an important port?

3. Which British Defence Secretary resigned over the Westland affair in 1986?

4. Arch, whorl and loops are all parts of what?

5. How many cards in a tarot pack?

Question Time 114

1. What is another name for tetanus?

2. Where in Ireland are the North and South Slobs?

3. Kelts, alevins and grilse are all forms of what?

4. What part did Sir Alec Guinness play in the film *The Bridge on the River Kwai*?

5. What colour is a giraffe's tongue?

Answers on page 121

Question Time 115

1. Name the English composer whose works include the *Enigma Variations*.

2. What substance forms an atoll?

3. Who made the first dynamo?

4. How many official horse race courses are there in Ireland?

5. What is Spanish for black?

Question Time 116

1. What does 'rabbi' actually mean?

2. Who discovered Brazil?

3. Which political party does Rev. Ian Paisley lead?

4. What were Liberty ships?

5. In which country would you find the Dordogne?

Question Time 117

1. What does 'Messiah' actually mean?

2. Sepia is a shade of what colour?

3. What do the initials of the political party SDLP stand for?

4. Which historic US monument is housed in Independence Hall, Philadelphia?

5. Where in Northern Ireland would you find the grave of St Patrick?

Question Time 118

1. Who was the first president of the Executive Council (prime minister) of the Irish Free State?

2. Which British poet wrote 'Arms and the Boy'?

3. What sort of creature is a megapode?

4. What are gherkins?

5. How many players are there in a baseball team?

Answers on page 122

Question Time 119

1. What is marsh gas?

2. Which is the largest of the United Arab Emirates?

3. In which year was the Atlantic Charter declared?

4. What in art is 'intaglio'?

5. In which country is Maiden Castle?

Question Time 120

1. When did Charles Haughey become Taoiseach?

2. Is the Suez Canal longer than the Panama Canal?

3. What did L.E. Waterman invent?

4. Which country has a parliament called the Duma?

5. What is palynology?

Answers on page 122

Question Time 121

1. Who wrote 'White Christmas'?

2. In which novel would you find the Thought Police?

3. What is the state capital of Arkansas?

4. What colour is titian?

5. If a person had myopia, which problem would he or she have?

Question Time 122

1. What is a somnambulist?

2. Which British general won the Battle of Malplaquet?

3. For which Irish organisation do the initials IFA stand?

4. A BCG is a vaccination against which disease?

5. What is the main ingredient of mornay sauce?

Answers on page 123

Question Time 123

1. How many players on a hurling team?

2. According to the Bible, what was used to feed the five thousand?

3. Baton Rouge is the capital of which American state?

4. Who played opposite Meryl Streep in *Ironweed*?

5. Against which disease was the Salk vaccine developed?

Question Time 124

1. What is a fifth columnist?

2. Which British general won the Battle of Vimeiro?

3. What does OAU stand for?

4. What is the capital of Nicaragua?

5. Name the main ingredient of mead.

Answers on page 123

Question Time 125

1. What colour are the flowers of the hop plant?

2. Name the warm currents that moderate the temperature of Ireland?

3. What did you do if you took the king's shilling?

4. Which George Bernard Shaw play inspired *My Fair Lady*?

5. Depending on the full moon, Easter Sunday may fall between 22 March and which date?

Question Time 126

1. Chelsea, Bow and Spode are all types of what?

2. Which UK coins are still regularly struck in standard silver?

3. What is the legislative capital of South Africa?

4. Which game bird season runs from 1 October to 1 February?

5. Which sailing event did Italy win in 1995 with 112.958 points?

Answers on page 124

Question Time 127

1. What colour are the flowers of the marjoram plant?

2. What sort of food is Bombay Duck?

3. Which river runs through Colchester?

4. Who solved the crime in *Death on the Nile*?

5. Which Sunday is Low Sunday or Quasimodo Sunday?

Question Time 128

1. What is the occupation of a leprechaun?

2. Where is the marian shrine of Fatima?

3. Name the two bones of the forearm.

4. Name the Roman god of the sea.

5. Who was the first woman to be proclaimed Queen of England?

Answers on page 124

Question Time 129

1. Which part of the body is affected by otitis?

2. If food is described as 'impacto', what does this mean?

3. From which county did the Flight of the Earls take place?

4. What is a boomslang?

5. How many players are there in a basketball team?

Question Time 130

1. Which is the largest freshwater lake in Ireland?

2. Name the two bones of the lower leg.

3. Who was the Greek god of the sea?

4. Who was on the British throne at the outbreak of World War One?

5. Name Ireland's highest mountain.

Answers on page 125

Question Time 131

1. What is calcium oxide?

2. What is the capital of Bangladesh?

3. Which political leaders brought about the Atlantic Charter?

4. What in art is a nimbus?

5. What is the county town of Leitrim?

Question Time 132

1. What is the common name for the fish soup popular in New England?

2. By what name is the former colony of the Belgian Congo now known?

3. What plant, with a stem of up to one foot, and droopy, pale green flowers, has a stinking variety?

4. What were King Charles I's supporters called in the Civil War?

5. What is the collective name for the three branches of government in Ireland?

Answers on page 125

Question Time 133

1. Which famous violinist of Russian Jewish parentage was born in New York in 1916?

2. Name the imaginary line where the earth and sky meet.

3. Which statesman who died in 1527 gave his name to a word meaning unscrupulous political cunning?

4. In which county is Blarney Castle?

5. From what is the liqueur calvados made?

Question Time 134

1. What is the name of the village in New York?

2. Who wrote *Our Man in Havana*?

3. Who recorded 'Wherever I lay my hat'?

4. Who starred opposite Jeremy Irons in *The French Lieutenant's Woman*?

5. Who won the tennis gold medal in the Women's Singles at the 1992 Olympics?

Answers on page 126

Question Time 135

1. What do the initials ANC stand for?

2. What is your normal body temperature?

3. In which Dickens novel does Mr Bumble appear?

4. What is the capital of Bolivia?

5. Where did Elvis Presley die?

Question Time 136

1. Which contender won the most gold medals in any Olympics?

2. When is Mardi Gras held?

3. With which unit is heat measured?

4. What divides Niagara Falls between Canada and the United States?

5. Who won the tennis gold medal in the Men's Singles at the 1992 Olympics?

Answers on page 126

Question Time 137

1. Who wrote the music for *West Side Story*?

2. What was Elvis Presley's middle name?

3. Who wrote the poem 'Dover Beach'?

4. In what year was the Bay of Pigs invasion?

5. What is a Havana brown?

Question Time 138

1. What language does a gypsy speak?

2. From which part of the pig does ham come?

3. What is meant by a fortified wine?

4. Who is protected by the Swiss Guards?

5. Which British spy died in Moscow in March 1983?

Answers on page 127

Question Time 139

1. What language did Jesus Christ speak?

2. Which infamous prison was stormed on 14 July 1789?

3. On how many hills was the ancient city of Rome built?

4. The world's most famous diamond is Koh-i-Noor: what does it mean?

5. Raleigh is the capital of which American state?

Question Time 140

1. What is the name of the art of cutting shrubs into ornamental shapes?

2. Give the name of a written statement, sworn on oath to be true, usually in the presence of a lawyer.

3. What is Esperanto?

4. Which confection is made from almonds, eggs and sugar?

5. In the book of Genesis, what was the intention in building the Tower of Babel?

Answers on page 127

Question Time 141

1. What is the feast day of St Bernard?

2. Where in Ireland would you find The Bull, The Cow and The Calf?

3. In which city is the International Atomic Energy Agency headquarters?

4. What term is used to define a woman before she is married?

5. How many sides has a pentagon?

Question Time 142

1. Which liquid might be described as corked?

2. Which two elements are combined to make common salt?

3. What are marmosets?

4. In which country is the Mekong river delta?

5. For his part in which TV programme did Rowan Atkinson win the Golden Rose of Montreux?

Answers on page 128

Question Time 143

1. What is the square root of a gross?

2. What element is added to steel to make it stainless?

3. What are marmots?

4. Which river flows into a vast swamp called the Sudd?

5. According to the old rhyme, the child of which day of the week has far to go?

Question Time 144

1. What nationality was Christopher Columbus?

2. Nowadays, who would regularly wear a wimple?

3. What, after potatoes, is the main ingredient of champ?

4. Which architects designed the British Houses of Parliament?

5. Who according to Greek mythology was the first woman?

Question Time 145

1. Name the Supreme Commander of the Allied Forces in World War Two.

2. Which England cricket test player of the 1990s began his career in Zimbabwe?

3. In which town did Lowry paint his landscapes?

4. Who recorded 'Suicide Blonde'?

5. Who was the first man to orbit the earth?

Question Time 146

1. Where was the second atomic bomb dropped in World War Two?

2. Which US president abolished slavery?

3. What did Dr Samuel Johnson describe as a triumph of hope over experience?

4. Who founded Fianna Fáil?

5. Who was the first man to walk on the moon?

Answers on page 129

Question Time 147

1. Who did Alan Dukes replace as leader of the Fine Gael Party?

2. What do Americans call potato crisps?

3. Which painter had a blue period?

4. Who acquired Singapore for Britain?

5. How long does the pregnancy of a dog last?

Question Time 148

1. The novel *The Day of the Jackal* was about the attempted assassination of whom?

2. Why are horses exempt from quarantine?

3. Who designed the mini skirt?

4. Where is the Sugar Loaf Mountain?

5. On which date was American Independence Day?

Answers on page 129

Question Time 149

1. In the novel *Animal Farm*, which breed of animal took over the farm?

2. Where in America were the witch trials of 1692 held?

3. What is a bagel?

4. In which month is the Cheltenham Gold Cup run?

5. Which Dickens character said, 'If the law supposes that ... the law is a ass — a idiot'?

Question Time 150

1. Which comes first: thunder or lightning?

2. Who invented the ball-point pen?

3. Is a gorilla a type of monkey?

4. Which people wrote on sheets of papyrus?

5. What did Sir Alexander Fleming discover?

Answers on page 130

Question Time 151

1. According to the Bible, who were the elder sons of Adam and Eve?

2. A grasshopper has ears on its legs: true or false?

3. Which whip-wielding film hero is named after a US state?

4. In modern terms, what nationality were the Spartans?

5. The word 'shalom' means 'peace' in which language: Hebrew, Arabic or Japanese?

Question Time 152

1. What is alleged to happen in the Bermuda Triangle?

2. What is a sovereign coin made from?

3. What is the name of an elephant's long tooth?

4. Which of these snakes is not venomous: rattlesnake, boa constrictor or viper?

5. In which country do they use Baht?

Answers on page 130

Question Time 153

1. What type of travel is associated with Cape Canaveral?

2. How would you get a hen's egg into a bottle without breaking the shell?

3. Who was assassinated on the Ides of March?

4. How many in a score?

5. The expression 'alternating current' refers to which form of energy?

Question Time 154

1. Where was the new Scottish Parliament opened in 1999?

2. Which plant, used as a Christmas decoration, was regarded as sacred by the Druids?

3. How long does it take light to reach earth from the sun?

4. 'Adios' means 'Goodbye' in French, Italian or Spanish?

5. What is the difference between a meteor and a meteorite?

Answers on page 131

Question Time 155

1. What is the name for the study of the earth's surface?

2. Which are the two major political parties in the USA?

3. What is unusual about sandalwood?

4. What function did Mercury perform in Greek legend?

5. What is brine?

Question Time 156

1. What is the name of the continent which contains the South Pole?

2. What American plant is both addictive for, and injurious to horses?

3. Which is further north: Turkey or Switzerland?

4. What game do the Chicago Bulls play?

5. If you flick a coin, what are the odds of it coming down heads?

Answers on page 131

Question Time 157

1. Is the earth a perfect sphere?

2. Which animals are thought to commit mass suicide by hurling themselves into the sea?

3. Why can't we see around corners?

4. Where in a house would you expect to find the eaves?

5. What name is given to ancient Egyptian writing?

Question Time 158

1. Shinto is the national religion of which country?

2. Is there more or less water now than when the seas were first formed?

3. What are young geese called?

4. By what name did Westerners formerly know Beijing?

5. What is the difference between astrology and astronomy?

Answers on page 132

Question Time 159

1. A chihuahua is a breed of what?

2. In the northern hemisphere, which wind would you expect to be colder: the north or the south?

3. Which country is the home of the classical guitar?

4. How many years are there in three score and ten?

5. What sort of creature could be described as a thoroughbred, a Shetland, an Arab or a Mustang?

Question Time 160

1. Which is the commonest gas in the atmosphere?

2. Where was golf invented?

3. According to the Beaufort scale, is a storm stronger than a gale?

4. How many movements are there usually in a classical symphony?

5. What is the first letter of the Greek alphabet?

Answers on page 132

Question Time 161

1. Who was principally responsible for the rise of National Socialism in Germany?

2. The first is Faith: what are the other graces?

3. What is glaciation?

4. From which flower is opium produced?

5. Name the first book of the Bible.

Question Time 162

1. What is the descriptive name for all species of pine tree?

2. Size for size, spider silk is stronger than steel: true or false?

3. What drink is flavoured with hops?

4. What does the Richter scale measure?

5. How many is a gross?

Answers on page 133

Question Time 163

1. What is a spring tide?

2. Which old lady guards Upper New York Bay?

3. Which complex character in Greek legend killed his father and married his mother?

4. In which revolution was Emiliano Zapata an important figure?

5. Who write *Lord of the Flies*?

Question Time 164

1. What is humidity?

2. Name the American inventor of the Kodak camera.

3. What does so-called 'natural gas' mainly comprise?

4. Which Roman emperor is supposed to have said, 'I came, I saw, I conquered'?

5. Against which Iraqi dictator was the Gulf War fought?

Answers on page 133

Question Time 165

1. What is the name given to the earth's hard outer shell?

2. Name the Egyptian queen who was the lover of Mark Anthony.

3. In which country would you find the Sinai Desert?

4. Name the Chinese leader of the Communist Revolution.

5. Which country first sent rhubarb to the West?

Question Time 166

1. The American, British and French flags have something in common. What is it?

2. What is azure?

3. Which country uses Roubles as its currency?

4. What are the colours of the rainbow?

5. What was the Soviet Army called?

Answers on page 134

Question Time 167

1. Name the colourful heroine associated with *Gone with the Wind*.

2. What colour uniforms did the opposing sides wear in the American Civil War?

3. What is the name of fast-flowing water found near rapids?

4. What is a zeppelin?

5. You could buy a Model T in only one colour: what was it?

Question Time 168

1. What do we call the metallic centre of the earth?

2. Name the hero of *The Hobbit*.

3. What is the main constituent of risotto?

4. Name the communist revolutionary, later prime minister then president of Cuba.

5. We say 'As blind as a bat', but is a bat really blind?

Answers on page 134

Question Time 169

1. What is strange about the Mediterranean Sea?

2. Which mythical Greek hero performed twelve labours?

3. What do we call a dense cloud of water droplets close to the ground?

4. What colour is saffron?

5. What do Australians call the uncultivated parts of their country?

Question Time 170

1. Which cat is considered lucky in some countries and an evil omen in others?

2. A blue flame indicates the presence of what metal?

3. Which three forms of power have been used to drive trains?

4. Which country is famous for growing tulips?

5. Does tea contain caffeine?

Answers on page 135

Question Time 171

1. What do we call a gap in the earth's crust through which molten rock escapes onto the earth's surface?

2. To which family do lions, tigers and cheetahs belong?

3. What sort of boat is a punt?

4. Which blackbird is not black: male or female?

5. Which country is the home of the game of boules?

Question Time 172

1. Name the largest species of predatory shark.

2. Which country has a security organisation called MI5?

3. Are giant pandas herbivores?

4. In which country did the Khmer Rouge carry out mass murder?

5. For which sport is Andre Agassi famous?

Answers on page 135

Question Time 173

1. Which two countries dispute ownership of Cyprus?

2. How much of the human body is composed of oxygen?

3. How do you judge the age of a tree which has been felled?

4. Where in China are the famous terracotta warriors?

5. Who wrote *The Four Seasons*?

Question Time 174

1. Where would you pay in Shekels?

2. Which female detective partners Fox Mulder in *The X-Files*?

3. Which nut is named after a South American country?

4. What sort of illness does a paediatrician treat?

5. What caused the *Titanic* to sink?

Answers on page 136

Question Time 175

1. Where is a country house known as a dacha?

2. What is tequila?

3. Who played the film role of Mary Poppins?

4. What is the national symbol of Ireland?

5. What have currants, raisins and sultanas got in common?

Answers

Question Time 1
1. Four
2. Antrim, Armagh, Down, Fermanagh, Derry, Tyrone
3. Lieutenant General
4. Fender Stratocaster
5. Cana of Galilee

Question Time 2
1. November 1963
2. Dubai
3. Charles Schulz (for 'Peanuts')
4. *Othello*
5. Red, yellow and blue

Question Time 3
1. W.B. Yeats, George Bernard Shaw, Samuel Beckett, Seamus Heaney
2. Aurora Borealis
3. Bill Gates and Paul Allen
4. The throat
5. Green

Question Time 4
1. Thirty-two
2. Russia
3. David O. Selznick
4. Catamaran
5. Jack Nicklaus (18 wins)

Question Time 5
1. Atlanta, Georgia
2. Elliot
3. Ramsay MacDonald
4. The shamrock
5. Karol Wojtyla

Question Time 6
1. James Connolly and Patrick Pearse
2. Isaac Asimov
3. Europe
4. Sir Walter Scott
5. Stuffs dead animals

Question Time 7
1. Stale
2. Chinese, English, Hindi, Spanish
3. Diamond
4. 'Puppet on a String'
5. Ernest Rutherford

Question Time 8
1. Greenland
2. *Ulysses*
3. 1977
4. Robert Peary (in 1909)
5. Pear

Question Time 9
1. Vladimir and Estragon
2. Uruguay (in 1930)
3. Morocco
4. On Air Force 1, Dallas (after the assassination of President John F. Kennedy)
5. John Paul I (in 1978)

Question Time 10
1. I am the Lord thy God. Thou shalt not have any false gods before Me.
2. Soviet Union
3. The Mont Blanc tunnel (under the Alps)
4. Percy Bysshe Shelley
5. Canberra

Question Time 11
1. Evolution
2. Venus
3. John Deere
4. Marathon
5. Soya-bean curd

Question Time 12
1. Tomato
2. A cathedral
3. Germaine Greer
4. New Zealand
5. Two

Question Time 13
1. The meek
2. The leek
3. Galway
4. The Penguin
5. The Washington Monument

Question Time 14
1. The Vatican
2. 'Brothers in Arms'
3. *Pride and Prejudice*
4. Joan of Arc
5. Alaska

Question Time 15
1. Shrove Tuesday
2. County Antrim
3. New York City
4. The whale shark
5. Census

Question Time 16
1. Capricorn
2. Ohio, Oklahoma, Oregon
3. Nine
4. Gold
5. Mozart

Question Time 17
1. The Massif Central and Pyrenees
2. Goat
3. Carbon monoxide
4. Jews
5. Bonnie Prince Charlie

Question Time 18
1. Double bass
2. Curling
3. Four
4. Dog
5. Switzerland

Question Time 19
1. 1949
2. India
3. A bird
4. Forty
5. Munster

Question Time 20
1. One kilogram
2. Roman Catholicism
3. Gymnastics
4. William Bateson
5. 4,500 million years

Question Time 21
1. Gabriel Fahrenheit
2. Mercedes Benz car
3. Listowel
4. A leap
5. Clare, Cork, Kerry, Limerick, Tipperary, Waterford

Question Time 22
1. World War II
2. *The Spirit of St Louis*
3. Scotland
4. Alexander Fleming
5. Dog

Question Time 23
1. Trafalgar
2. Lester Piggot
3. Clare
4. Paul Simon
5. Hare

Question Time 24
1. Marilyn Monroe
2. Yes (cream cheese)
3. Nine minutes
4. Fifteen
5. Nanosecond

Question Time 25
1. The Derby
2. The Moon
3. Speedy Gonzales
4. Saturday, after Saturn
5. John Cleese

Question Time 26
1. Buttercup
2. Cusack, Hogan, Nally
3. Juan Fangio
4. East to west
5. Acetic acid

Question Time 27
1. 1961
2. Eagle
3. Moulin Rouge
4. Crete
5. Douglas Hyde

Question Time 28
1. William (of Orange) and James II
2. Twelve
3. Spanish
4. Roald Amundsen
5. Louisa May Alcott

Question Time 29
1. Drogheda
2. Clement Attlee
3. Madrid
4. Alexander Solzhenitsyn
5. A bird

Question Time 30
1. *Lord of the Rings*
2. Hudson
3. James Brown
4. True
5. St Teresa of Avila

Question Time 31
1. Ottawa
2. Tea
3. Washington
4. Beethoven
5. The weasel family

Question Time 32
1. New Zealand
2. Churchill Downs
3. A semitone
4. St James
5. 1989

Question Time 33
1. Southern
2. A form
3. Britain and China
4. Antonio
5. Honolulu

Question Time 34
1. Gerald Ford
2. Prix de l'Arc de Triomphe
3. A bat
4. David Livingstone
5. 15 July

Question Time 35
1. John F. Kennedy
2. Circumference
3. USA
4. Othello
5. Sacramento

Question Time 36
1. James Callaghan
2. Andrew Morton
3. A monkey
4. Sudan
5. May

Question Time 37
1. Neapolitan
2. Plato
3. Hilary, Easter, Trinity, Michaelmas
4. Textiles
5. Edvard Munch

Question Time 38
1. Three
2. A beggar
3. Ironsides
4. Proper names
5. Mead

Question Time 39
1. County Kildare
2. It was waterproof
3. Beefeaters
4. Sugar
5. Belief in one god

Question Time 40
1. First past the post
2. The Flying Dutchman
3. *The Knight's Tale*
4. Foxglove
5. Essex

Question Time 41
1. Maize
2. $13^1/_2$ inches
3. False (Franz Hals)
4. Ontario and Erie
5. Fourteen

Question Time 42
1. The Gulf of Mexico
2. 'Over the hills and far away'
3. Paddington (London)
4. New York City
5. The palms of the hands and the soles of the feet

Question Time 43
1. Lapland
2. Nine days old
3. Christine Keeler
4. Violin
5. Tooth enamel

Question Time 44
1. Ecuador
2. Potatoes
3. Fashion designer
4. The sound barrier
5. Seventy-eight feet (23.77 m)

Question Time 45
1. Argentina
2. James
3. Cheese
4. 'Solitude' (by Ella Wheeler Wilcox)
5. Three feet (91.4 cm)

Question Time 46
1. True
2. Horse hair
3. Colorado
4. Biopsy
5. MM

Question Time 47
1. Lady
2. Turkey
3. St Petersburg (Leningrad)
4. Thirty-five to one
5. Ganges

Question Time 48
1. Queensland
2. Two
3. Greece
4. Dame Ninette de Valois
5. Ten

Question Time 49
1. Memory
2. Sculpture
3. Francis Ford Coppola
4. World War II
5. Prometheus

Question Time 50
1. Blood
2. Lake Titicaca
3. China
4. Vincent Van Gogh
5. Influenza

Question Time 51
1. Charles I
2. Rugby
3. John McGahern
4. Lungs
4. The Po

Question Time 52
1. Apollo Eleven
2. Joseph Stalin
3. The Wonderbra
4. Malta
5. U2

Question Time 53
1. Baritone
2. Cabbage
3. Hamnet
4. Denmark
5. Indianapolis

Question Time 54
1. T.S. Eliot
2. Antrim
3. *The Picture of Dorian Gray*
4. Dick van Dyke
5. American

Question Time 55
1. Up
2. Michael Flatley
3. Ernest Hemingway
4. California
5. Light

Question Time 56
1. Vatican City
2. Freetown
3. A bomber
4. Patrick Sarsfield
5. Himalaya

Question Time 57
1. Catherine Cookson
2. Dublin
3. Hans Christian Andersen
4. Dumplings of potatoes, flour or semolina
5. Apache

Question Time 58
1. Ants
2. Kingston
3. France
4. Forty-three
5. *The Dandy*

Question Time 59
1. The Acts of the Apostles
2. Eight
3. 1916
4. Elm
5. John Logie Baird

Question Time 60
1. Six
2. The mast nearest the stern
3. Cain, Abel and Seth
4. Seven
5. Zambia

Question Time 61
1. The Sam Maguire Cup
2. Duodenum
3. Two
4. Cuchulainn
5. Death Valley, California

Question Time 62
1. Twenty-six
2. Louis de Bernières
3. Cork
4. Secretary of State
5. 1910

Question Time 63
1. Riga
2. A heavy draught horse
3. Six
4. John Boorman
5. Left

Question Time 64
1. *Sense and Sensibility*
2. Twelve
3. Five
4. In a church
5. Ulster Defence Regiment

Question Time 65
1. 150
2. Dictionaries
3. Aspirin
4. Pete Sampras
5. Through their skin

Question Time 66
1. Catherine (of Aragon)
2. Cataract
3. Purdah
4. Jonathan Swift
5. The liver

Question Time 67
1. Ophelia's
2. In the neck
3. Jihad
4. Irwin Shaw
5. Gary Kasparov

Question Time 68
1. A card game
2. Blood
3. A long spoon
4. Hymns
5. Heinrich Himmler

Question Time 69
1. Forget-me-not
2. In a library. (It is a system of classifying books.)
3. St Paul
4. Birr, Co. Offaly
5. Meccano

Question Time 70
1. A coin
2. Dr Samuel Johnson
3. Twenty-six
4. Fair Isle
5. Marie Stopes

Question Time 71
1. Hyacinth
2. In the sky. They are a group of stars.
3. William Shakespeare
4. Kilkenny
5. Belgium

Question Time 72
1. Elvis Costello
2. Double-think
3. Twelve
4. Banshee
5. Tower of London

Question Time 73
1. Eighteen
2. Redingote
3. A rock climber
4. 'La Marseillaise'
5. Master of the Rolls

Question Time 74
1. 1955
2. Gaberdine
3. Tug-of-war or rowing
4. 1984
5. My Lord

Question Time 75
1. Tagus
2. Gross Domestic Product
3. Its wall game
4. La Mancha
5. Beaver

Question Time 76
1. River Moskva
2. Polish
3. Marriage
4. Henry Fielding
5. Jealousy

Question Time 77
1. Exodus
2. Albany
3. President Richard Nixon
4. Cactusville
5. North Island, New Zealand

Question Time 78
1. Hydrology
2. In your throat at the back of your mouth
3. William Pitt, first Earl of Chatham
4. Crete
5. *Mansfield Park* by Jane Austen

Question Time 79
1. Metallurgy
2. Cologne
3. Mary Shelley
4. Brands Hatch
5. Zürich

Question Time 80
1. Deuteronomy
2. Thabo Mbeki
3. Crabs
4. A pocket watch
5. Two over par for a hole

Question Time 81
1. The feeding of the five thousand
2. The Norwegian krone
3. A snake
4. Braemar
5. A pig

Question Time 82
1. Thirty-five
2. The Queen of Hearts in *Alice in Wonderland*
3. Henry Carey
4. Oliver
5. Just before dawn

Question Time 83
1. Christmas Day
2. *Tess of the d'Urbervilles*
3. George and Ira Gershwin
4. Jefferson
5. Winston Churchill

Question Time 84
1. *Macbeth*
2. A hog
3. The bicycle
4. The dollar
5. A bat

Question Time 85
1. *Twelfth Night*
2. A jenny
3. The Montgolfier brothers
4. The dinar
5. A diving sea-duck

Question Time 86
1. The Scaffold
2. Jesse Owens
3. Abraham
4. Richard Nixon
5. The Battle of Waterloo

Question Time 87
1. St Helena
2. Cheese
3. The hair
4. John Cabot
5. Caustic soda

Question Time 88
1. The Bible
2. Argentina
3. A jumper
4. Zsa Za Gabor
5. A poet

Question Time 89
1. Intestines
2. Oysters
3. Luton Town
4. Mainz
5. Epsom salts

Question Time 90
1. Herman Wouk
2. 30 November
3. *Moby Dick*
4. He invented the flush toilet
5. A computer which beat world champion Gary Kasparov

Question Time 91
1. Darwin
2. The IRA
3. Puccini
4. Terence Conran
5. A joey

Question Time 92
1. Sammy Davis Jnr
2. John F. Kennedy
3. A cat
4. Tchaikovsky
5. Roulette

Question Time 93
1. James Gandon
2. Four
3. Santiago
4. November to April
5. The sun

Question Time 94
1. David Soul
2. The corona
3. A bloody Mary
4. Graham Hill
5. The rattlesnake

Question Time 95
1. Colleen McCullough
2. Bay
3. *Twelfth Night*
4. The bodhi tree
5. A swimming pool

Question Time 96
1. A missionary
2. *Four Weddings and a Funeral*
3. The Ombudsman
4. L'Escargot
5. Turin

Question Time 97
1. Bob Hope
2. James Monroe; the capital is Monrovia
3. Tunisia
4. United States
5. Fifteen

Question Time 98
1. Rooster
2. Tom Hanks
3. Kentucky
4. G.K. Chesterton
5. Karl Marx

Question Time 99
1. Elizabeth
2. Hanoi
3. Pope
4. A prison
5. The kiwi

Question Time 100
1. Jules Rimet
2. Venice
3. Polo
4. Trousers
5. Thomas Mann

Question Time 101
1. Jutland
2. John Hurt
3. Spanish
4. Salisbury Cathedral
5. South-west of Sri Lanka, in the Indian Ocean

Question Time 102
1. Kublai Khan
2. Robert Wagner
3. Romulus
4. Palaeontology
5. Thrush

Question Time 103
1. The North-West Passage
2. Architecture
3. Friday (after Frig)
4. Ecology
5. The US/Mexican border

Question Time 104
1. The Three Degrees
2. Pluto
3. Dom Perignon
4. Jackie Stewart
5. The giraffe

Question Time 105
1. Cordelia
2. An alcoholic
3. Geneva
4. A horse
5. Alcoholics Anonymous

Question Time 106
1. Edward Lear
2. A vacuum
3. Haka
4. India
5. A body

Question Time 107
1. Vanessa Redgrave
2. Italy and Austria
3. Spain
4. Callaghan
5. Mary II

Question Time 108
1. Polish
2. Eighteen
3. Jules Verne
4. John Huston
5. Jeroboam

Question Time 109
1. A cat
2. North Sea
3. William Hunt
4. Toyland
5. Port-of-Spain

Question Time 110
1. You would vomit
2. Ecuador, Colombia, Brazil
3. Groucho, Chico, Harpo, Zeppo, Gummo
4. *The Muppet Show*
5. George V

Question Time 111
1. Ash Wednesday
2. One
3. Actors
4. Roman Polanski
5. Champagne

Question Time 112
1. Stonefish
2. William Shakespeare
3. Bavaria
4. Bedrock
5. The original thirteen colonies

Question Time 113
1. Leprosy
2. Chile
3. Michael Heseltine
4. Fingerprints
5. Seventy-eight

Question Time 114
1. Lockjaw
2. County Wexford
3. Salmon
4. Colonel Nicholson
5. Blue

Question Time 115
1. Edward Elgar
2. Coral
3. Michael Faraday
4. Twenty-seven
5. Negro

Question Time 116
1. My master
2. Pedro Alvarez Cabral
3. Democratic Unionist Party
4. Cargo vessels built during World War Two as part of the US war effort
5. France

Question Time 117
1. Anointed, or the anointed one
2. Brown
3. Social Democratic and Labour Party
4. The Liberty Bell
5. Downpatrick

Question Time 118
1. W.T. Cosgrave
2. Wilfred Owen
3. An Australian game bird
4. Cucumbers
5. Nine

Question Time 119
1. Methane
2. Abu Dhabi
3. 1941
4. An engraved design cut into a hollow (the opposite of a cameo)
5. Dorset, England

Question Time 120
1. 11 December 1979
2. Yes, it's twice as long
3. The fountain pen
4. Russia
5. The study of spores and pollen

Question Time 121
1. Irving Berlin
2. *1984*
3. Little Rock
4. Red
5. Short-sightedness

Question Time 122
1. A sleep-walker
2. Duke of Marlborough
3. Irish Farmers Association
4. Tuberculosis
5. Cheese

Question Time 123
1. Fifteen
2. Bread and fish
3. Louisiana
4. Jack Nicholson
5. Polio

Question Time 124
1. A member of a subversive group
2. Duke of Wellington
3. Organisation of African Unity
4. Managua
5. Honey

Question Time 125
1. Yellow and green
2. The Gulf Stream
3. Joined the army
4. *Pygmalion*
5. 25 April

Question Time 126
1. Porcelain
2. Maundy money
3. Cape Town
4. Pheasant
5. The Admiral's Cup

Question Time 127
1. Rose and purple
2. A fish
3. River Colne
4. Hercule Poirot
5. The first Sunday after Easter

Question Time 128
1. Cobbler
2. Portugal
3. Radius and ulna
4. Neptune
5. Lady Jane Grey

Question Time 129
1. The ear
2. Breaded
3. Donegal
4. A snake
5. Five

Question Time 130
1. Lough Neagh
2. Fibula and tibia
3. Poseidon
4. George V
5. Carrantouhill

Question Time 131
1. Lime
2. Dhaka
3. Franklin D. Roosevelt and Winston Churchill
4. A halo of light painted over a holy figure
5. Carrick-on-Shannon

Question Time 132
1. Chowder
2. Democratic Republic of Congo (formerly Zaire)
3. Hellebore
4. Cavaliers
5. The Oireachtas

Question Time 133
1. Yehudi Menuhin
2. The horizon
3. Machiavelli
4. Cork
5. Apples

Question Time 134
1. Greenwich Village
2. Graham Greene
3. Paul Young
4. Meryl Streep
5. Jennifer Capriati

Question Time 135
1. African National Congress
2. 37 degrees C or 98.6 degrees F
3. *Oliver Twist*
4. La Paz
5. Memphis, Tennessee

Question Time 136
1. Nadia Comaneci
2. Shrove Tuesday
3. A therm
4. Goat Island
5. Marc Rosset

Question Time 137
1. Leonard Bernstein
2. Aaron
3. Matthew Arnold
4. 1961
5. A breed of small rabbit

Question Time 138
1. Romany
2. Hind leg
3. One strengthened with added alcohol
4. The pope
5. Donald Maclean

Question Time 139
1. Aramaic
2. The Bastille
3. Seven
4. Mountain of light
5. North Carolina

Question Time 140
1. Topiary
2. Affidavit
3. An artificial language
4. Marzipan
5. It was supposed to reach heaven

Question Time 141
1. 16 May
2. They are islands off Dursey Head on the Beara Peninsula, Co. Cork
3. Vienna
4. Spinster
5. Five

Question Time 142
1. Wine
2. Sodium and chlorine
3. Small monkeys
4. (South) Vietnam
5. *Mr Bean*

Question Time 143
1. Twelve
2. Chromium
3. Rodents of the squirrel family
4. The White Nile (in the Sudan)
5. Thursday

Question Time 144
1. Italian
2. A nun
3. Scallions
4. Sir Charles Barry and A.W. Pugin
5. Pandora

Question Time 145
1. Dwight D. Eisenhower
2. Graham Hick
3. Salford
4. INXS
5. Yuri Gagarin

Question Time 146
1. Nagasaki
2. Abraham Lincoln
3. A second marriage
4. Éamon de Valera
5. Neil Armstrong

Question Time 147
1. Garret FitzGerald
2. Potato chips
3. Pablo Picasso
4. Sir Thomas Stanford Raffles
5. Nine weeks

Question Time 148
1. Charles de Gaulle
2. They cannot pass rabies to humans
3. Mary Quant
4. County Wicklow
5. 4 July 1776

Question Time 149
1. Pigs
2. Salem, Massachusetts
3. A leavened bread roll shaped like a doughnut
4. March
5. Mr Bumble

Question Time 150
1. Lightning
2. Ladislao Biro
3. No, it's an ape
4. The ancient Egyptians
5. Penicillin

Question Time 151
1. Cain and Abel
2. True
3. Indiana Jones
4. Greek
5. Hebrew

Question Time 152
1. The strange disappearance of ships and aircraft
2. Gold
3. A tusk
4. Boa constrictor
5. Thailand

Question Time 153
1. Space travel
2. Soak it in vinegar to soften the shell
3. Julius Caesar
4. Twenty
5. Electricity

Question Time 154
1. Edinburgh
2. Mistletoe
3. Eight minutes
4. Spanish
5. A meteor remains in space whereas a meteorite survives contact with our atmosphere and strikes the ground.

Question Time 155
1. Geography
2. Republicans and Democrats
3. It smells sweet
4. He was a messenger of the gods
5. Salt water

Question Time 156
1. Antarctica
2. Loco weed
3. Switzerland
4. Basketball
5. Evens

Question Time 157
1. No
2. Lemmings
3. Because light travels in straight lines
4. In the roof
5. Hieroglyphics

Question Time 158
1. Japan
2. Neither! There is exactly the same amount.
3. Goslings
4. Peking
5. Astrology studies the influence of the stars on human behaviour. Astronomy is the scientific observation of cosmic phenomena.

Question Time 159
1. Dog
2. The north wind
3. Spain
4. Seventy
5. A horse

Question Time 160
1. Nitrogen
2. Scotland
3. No
4. Four
5. Alpha

Question Time 161
1. Adolf Hitler
2. Hope and Charity
3. The covering of land by ice during the Ice Age
4. The poppy
5. Genesis

Question Time 162
1. Coniferous
2. True
3. Beer
4. The magnitude of an earthquake
5. One hundred and forty-four

Question Time 163
1. An especially high or low tide
2. The Statue of Liberty
3. Oedipus
4. The Mexican Revolution
5. William Golding

Question Time 164
1. The amount of water vapour in the air
2. George Eastman
3. Methane
4. Julius Caesar
5. Saddam Hussein

Question Time 165
1. The crust
2. Cleopatra
3. Egypt
4. Mao Zedong
5. China

Question Time 166
1. They are all red, white and blue
2. A shade of blue
3. Russia
4. Red, orange, yellow, green, blue, indigo, violet
5. The Red Army

Question Time 167
1. Scarlett O'Hara
2. Blue and grey
3. White water
4. A rigid airship
5. Black

Question Time 168
1. The core
2. Bilbo Baggins
3. Rice
4. Fidel Castro
5. No, but it has poor sight

Question Time 169
1. It has no tides
2. Hercules
3. Fog (or mist)
4. Yellow
5. The outback

Question Time 170
1. A black cat
2. Copper
3. Steam, diesel, electricity
4. The Netherlands (Holland)
5. Yes

Question Time 171
1. A volcano
2. The cat family
3. An open flat-bottomed boat propelled by a long pole and used in shallow waters
4. The female
5. France

Question Time 172
1. The Great White
2. Great Britain
3. Mainly, but they will eat meat when they get it
4. Cambodia
5. Tennis

Question Time 173
1. Greece and Turkey
2. Approximately two-thirds
3. By the number of concentric rings in the trunk
4. Xi'an
5. Antonio Vivaldi

Question Time 174
1. Israel
2. Dana Scully
3. A Brazil
4. Children's diseases
5. It struck an iceberg

Question Time 175
1. Russia
2. A Mexican spirit brewed from cactus
3. Julie Andrews
4. A harp
5. They are all types of dried grape